Library of Sandwiches

by Pat Smith

Library of Sandwiches

Poems by
Pat Smith

Brooklyn, New York

All rights reserved.
No part of this book may be produced in any form
without written permission of the copyright owner.

ISBN: 978-0-578-40279-6
ISBN/SKU: 9780578402796

Cover design by: Simon Smith
Book design: Esther K. Smith
Design production: Rabia Hussain

© 2018 Patrick Smith

Brooklyn, New York

To Sue

Contents

8	Penny in the Subway
10	Something Else
11	Bugged
12	Invitation to a Masquerade
13	Tonight at Ten
14	Ulysses Ossuary
15	In Confidence
16	Library of Sandwiches
17	Uncle Who
18	Countdown
19	This Duck
20	Beta Agonists
21	Buttons
22	Big Shadow, Small Mirror
23	Aqueous or Celestial
24	Tergiversations of Lux Delite
26	My Sin
27	How I Feel About Cigars
28	His Car, His Bed, His Christmas Tree
29	Obsessive, The Cowboy
30	The View from Sturges Corner
32	In The Mountains
33	Janus in Pajamas
34	Dear Tomorrow
35	Voiceover Artist

36	Wintry Mix
37	At Her Service
38	Or Dusty, Depending
39	My Man Sydney
40	One Ring Circus
41	Your Faithful Observer
42	You Might
43	Agar Agar Flipped Me Out
44	Summer Monday
45	A Little Radioactive Cube of Black
46	Harvest of Hail
47	New Season
48	Battery Gardens
49	Sometimes
50	In Exurbia
51	Make It Old
52	For Sue
53	Who Knew
54	Liberty Ashes
55	Later That Afternoon
56	Another Day in Paradise
57	Leonard
58	To My New Pal Li Po
59	Jupiter
60	Urgent
61	Wichita Lineman Sutra

Penny in the Subway

I stumbled into a museum of waiting
Before I could be edified
The nerds in charge had me looking
For a stupid thread from a narrow ladder
To upholstered anterooms
Where I spotted a spool on the carpet
Thank god and beat it out of there.
I didn't care it turned out to be twine.
I could wait without supervision.

It took me so long to get into costume
I completely missed my entrance
Because first I had to take off my eight shirts
And I was amazed to see that the soles of my feet
Instead of being mostly smooth as I'd always thought
Were in fact a cabbage-like forest of pink flesh
Folds upon folds that unfurled to reveal hidden recesses.
Sure I was a little creeped out but

When they say be my guest I'm always there
Tip-toeing down the hall to a tastefully tiled bathroom
Where a state of the art toilet
Regards me with barely veiled contempt.
What's for breakfast, I ask my suspiciously smiling friends
As they make for the street in their coats.
Oh cousin Jane has sautéed some greens.
They sit in the pan like leftover seaweed supper.

I hate this crappy beach resort anyway.
Hell I can't even find the beach
That's forever calling me back.
I punch in the numbers and get returned to a page
Where I punch in more numbers to an elevator
So grimy and tiny it dumps me in a back alley
I ride somebody's motorized wheelchair
Around the leaf strewn dusty poolside
And find a seagull skeleton

You can't just walk across stage now
Said the busybody actress everybody
Will see you I said relax baby the show
Is already a total disaster she said
Oh are you having a bad night too
Drink some water
She gave me a bottle with lots of names
On the label these are my nicknames
Did you have nicknames when you were little
One of mine was ankle bracelet
Quick let's go before Miss B kills us
I tried to pull my pile of pieces together
To sprint upstairs but all my socks kept rolling away

You could see right into her soul, Eddie
She was polished bronze
A muscled Michelangelo amazon
Arched in Urdhva Dhanurasana
Over a silver globe I fell in love
With the finely wrought drops of sweat
On her upper lip intended for the apex
Of some grand edifice
She was hanging out in a museum of waiting
I had to spring her somehow
A heads up penny brings no luck
If you don't bend down to pick it up

Something Else

I brought my baby's faded blanket
to a cheerful children's museum
to see if they could make it
into something else for me.
A former TV personality in candy
stripes and skimmer hat
met me to repurpose the past
as a snazzy shirt, an umbrella, maybe
a lot of fuzzy handkerchiefs.
How 'bout a superhero cape?
Too obvious. I was impatient
to cut a pattern, run it up,
put it on and move out
from under to go anywhere
I was bound to go but old
accordion Uncle Al didn't give
me my bundle back
once we got off the merry go round.
It became something else,
shadow, snapshot, sudden hurt
all by itself,
turning the corner on two strong legs

Bugged

May azaleas flat out flaunt their lipstick pinks
Duck out early from the office is what I do
They know your secrets, whispers a man
Wearing a sandwich sign for foot-long subs

Everybody knows my secrets, I say
I'm an open book with live bugs inside
He says, what do you know about vampire
Blankets my eye is black I don't know why

I say, I know just the spot for you to go
By the river things are singing crazy little licks
He says, pigeons shit all over the benches
Yet we're supposed to love them

How miraculous their spiraling flight, I say
As I pivot to make my escape
When a pathetic open-air tourist bus
Rides up rudely in front of us

Grampa, Grampa, oh my god!
Calls out an angel's voice like a bell
A tribe of sunburned bodhisattvas descends
From the upper deck, hugging and kissing

Nearly knocking him down with affection
They bundle him, weeping, onto the bus
That speeds them on to glories unknown
And leaves me agape, alone with his sign

That I wear to the open sky and graceful
frenzy of the bee-buzzing rhododendrons

Invitation to a Masquerade

To Tawn Earnest spokesman for Dollar General
And Summer Ash director of outreach
On the occasion of the Transit of Venus
Let me say upfront I love your names
And I invite you to come as a commedia clown
And her killer shadow
For game-used dirt from all thirty ballparks
Where we will scale outdoor sculpture
To deploy a mobile splicing unit
And bounce it off a donut fender
Darlings please don't overthink it
Yours sincerely King of Sleep
Répondez s'il vous plaît

P.S. the rectangular holes in my forehead
Are the latest eastern fashion
Perfectly cut voids, one big, one small
You can see the air right through them
The big one holds a shiny metal gizmo
That I think controls my gears
Until I pull back the blue plastic liner
To reveal a dark pond beneath my pool
And a startled puffer fish
Who I guess is me since I smoke
Segments of wrought iron fence

To install on summer cabin porches
And light your way with tiki torches

Tonight at Ten

We thought it was thunder when we woke
But cutting edge machines cut off
The front wall of our house and part of our roof

Turning our home into a reality theater
Below which the hardhat in charge
Instructed us to be careful at the edge. Across

The street the wall of the butcher's was also gone
So little boys could jump into piles of meat.
How did we feel, me, mom and the girls?

Confused but pretty chipper considering our neighbors
Had quite the view of us in our pajamas
So we pulled out the Scrabble© Uncertainty Edition

With the secret scores hidden on the bottom
The pieces of the puzzle board. Having no wall
We had to pay special attention

To the weather of course and it fell
To me to write a complete forecast on the belly
Of a remarkably obedient German shepherd

Rescue dog that lay there patiently but still
It was impossible to fit all the words on the map.
And the world was watching.

Ulysses Ossuary

I am Ulysses Ossuary, also known
as Barton Bone, part-time professional
ventriloquist. I throw my voice around
the house afraid of getting hollowed out.
I'm wary of the basement water
rising through the kitchen linoleum and
rivering out my open door. When thick
necked hardhats and the cracked
landlord inspect the suspect pipes I play
a sad croquet of wickets with impossible lips
and wonder about the broken hinges
on the box of shoes I don't wear anymore.

Do not advertise, admonishes my
Times, imaginary addresses for
temporary trailers with spread-eagled
eagles over the door. That's where
I picked up this rash on my ankle,
a carbuncled gem of multicolored dice.
I'm afraid my costume won't cover the sore.
Nor can I repair the busted axle on my
Model T Ford with coat hanger wire
and old cardboard. Moving vans arrive again
to bring me back where I've never been,
my childhood's recently renovated home.

In Confidence

I was at the wheel but the car drove me
Beside myself, spinning backwards
Bumping down marble stairs
To a garden party's rose colored martinis
And somebody's very entertaining baby
Till missing luggage and forgotten adapters
Induced the usual panic about our nervous devices
When the famously dead painter asked
What's it like to be responsible
For your own costumes and props

It ain't rocket surgery but
I dropped my sword down a sewer grate
Couldn't find a parking space
Circled around and over the hill
At each pass losing a shirt or a shoe
But comforted by the black and white stripes
Of a tug boat, a two-tone Orvieto cathedral
Pushing a rust iron hulk up the Hudson
To where it has fallen to me to repair
The broken icon of Saint Somebody
Patron of resolutely cheerful losers
His book, his crooked staff, his haloed head
All in pieces

Library Of Sandwiches

Most of our bodies were stuck
Under a table but we raised our heads
Up between an edge and a wall
Like characters in a Beckett tragicomedy.
A sweet smell of growing green things
Made my heart hurt a little, said Rocky.
I was a child, school was just out,
Nothing to worry about.
What would we do without perpective?
I said. I remember a crumbling tunnel
To a beach location of so many dreams.
Rocky said, May used to mean an impending surge
Of joy—sixth grade is over!
And loss—sixth grade is over.
What's May to me today?
What warm breeze?
What sexy trees?
What sweet possibilities?
I said, Maybe I wished I could be
In the quiet storefront office
The schoolbus went by every morning
Because I just wanted some calm, damn it.
We are vessels, are we not,
Of all that came before, said Rocky.
Happy in Grampa's Lap, watching Jackie Gleason,
Algebra homework, Revolver on the record player,
Knee-deep and laughing in warm ocean waves
With you, the one who saves my life.
How would I let you go? I said.
For an unusual tattoo I wanted
Something from a dream.
Though not a slice of rye
To cover a hole in my door
But mysterious enough to draw
Attention in yoga class:
Faint pink crystals scattered
Across a pale blue sky.
Can they do that?
Anything is possible, Rocky said.

Uncle Who

I wasn't always pursued by wolves
And the admonition to relax about it
I would find shiny whistles at whim
Listen to the whispering breeze
In the new oak leaves
Best in the western hemisphere, ok?
New part, new play
Late substitution
Impenetrable text
I am an Uncle who
Somehow saves the day
Former Navy captain, gay
I taste some sorbet, cross
To the couch, the assistant
Young, smart, blonde, she
Says, you can do this
Oh yeah, I say
Guideline buckets, orphan drugs
Positively impactful, but
The numbers don't roll, Skipper
A last-minute change of venue
Made my mom miss the show
To freely wander within the city walls of life
Without getting worried about work
To let go of the men's belt
That narrow strip of boring brown
Dumb and unnecessary
Fetish of antique uniforms
The wolves are always wearing
Oh, for omens of cosmic disorder
Crazy-ass abnormalities
Two-headed goats
Speckled trout from the sky
I lie down in the road
To piss off the world
From the pyramid's apex
I watch for my enemies
One true thing
One neat trick
One time only
One last chance

Countdown

As one's ectoplasm inevitably erodes
It's important to dress with pizzazz
Said the presiding spirit at my screen door
Antique prince, camouflage cummerbund
Himself the ghost of his own father
Puffing on five cigarettes at once
Killing time on lower Broadway
I carried a lost boy on my shoulders, he said
Midtown Manhattan, hard as glass
Collecting old toys in a milk crate
Looking for a window that lets you see
Not to harp on it but Uncle Johnny
Do you remember
Used to hoist us up to the roof
Of the outhouse so we could see
The 4th of July fireworks from LeSourdsville Lake
I guess I'm a bird
If I had to say
Albeit a clumsy one
Not Baudelaire's albatross
By any stretch
I mean I'm an okay dancer
But I have a raptor's eye
For unusual signage—
Scorpion Traffic Devices
Time Shred Services—
And an ear for the odd call—
A Thrasher's husky kooi-dwid
Before I lift off

This Duck

I closed my eyes against the glare
When I opened them a mallard stood
In the snow beside me, yellow beak shining
He settled down, sank his green head
Into the feathers on his back
Eyes on me slowly blinking closed

A blue police boat slowly closed in on us
I thought the cops might say something
Yes officers, I can vouch for this duck
This duck saved my life and could save yours someday
This duck knows how to meditate on snow like nobody's business
You may approach this duck with your thoughts and desires
But please respect the personal space of this duck

All the grinning pilot did was nose the prow against a piling
Again and again, to test it I guess
It woke up the duck

Beta Agonists

Please order food for today's conference, Roger said.
I said, Of course. And encrypt the message, he said.
Encrypt our lunch? I said. Send it secure, he said.
We need to be in full compliance. I said, I guess we can't
Be too careful. Especially about sandwiches.
I'm serious, Murchison, Roger said. I said, Me, too.
I don't take my pastrami lightly. He said, Pastrami—that gets out,
boom, total red flag. Code purple all over the place. I said,
Jesus. I had no idea. He said, investigators in our files, circling
like hyenas around the copy machine. I said, The bastards!
We'll shoot them down like dogs. Roger said, Whoa,
Murchison. I love my dog. I love all dogs. I said, Right, sorry.
I used to have a dog when I was a lad. What kind of
Sandwich do you want? I asked. Roger said,
That's protected information. Order a selection.
Roger left and a chill went straight through me.
One leak, tuna salad, and German shepherds
Are sniffing under my desk. I'd be out
On the street, aimless, wandering
Lonely as a cloud. And there goes my pension.

Buttons

I pushed a million buttons today
I couldn't call you
I couldn't get through
My screens were sepia seascapes
So tired I fell asleep
swimming alone in a sunny cove
Floating peaceful till uh-oh
Nobody knew where I was

I pushed a million buttons today
I swam through a sidewalk
I got stuck at a funeral
for my mother's kitchen stove
I pulled it together
I lined up the holes
I saw two lights shining
red and green at once
Stop or Go Christmas shop

I pushed a million buttons today
I saw armies of young women
in 50's retro one-piece gym suits
They carried carbine rifles
They patrolled suburban streets
Looking to shoot I don't know who

I pushed a million buttons today
I saw city kids in tombstone repose
I saw myself asleep in Grampa's barn
a gentle lion roared in my bed
It was the deep snore of my one true love

Big Shadow, Small Mirror

To cut the grass by Maggie's garden path
I haul my electric mower through a grocery,
climb a gothic arch, dangle from a flying buttress
but there's nowhere to plug in.
Maggie blithely takes the top off the mower,
puts in newspaper, charcoal, lights it
and pours on gasoline.
I say, Hey, that's dangerous!
She says it rarely causes problems.

My consultant says it's time to minimize
optionality and variation so there's no way
to tweak the system. I say, Cookbook medicine.
He says it's just something to be aware of.
I say, Sauce for the gander. We meet
all those risk corridors. He says if
something's out of whack you have a potential
case. I say, Strategic default done right.
He says he slept in a car outside the office.
I say, Tiffany Fur Storage?
He says John Fish Jewelers.
I say, Partial, fractional and promised gifts.
He says rival girl groups threatened
by the Russian mob. I say, A Traveler's Guide
to Cloud People.

As for her concern over her perfume's staying power,
she still smelled great when I made sure
she was breathing and I waited for the EMTs.

Aqueous or Celestial

In a regrettable act of kindness
mixed with curiosity
I cut loose an old man shrink
wrapped in red plastic,
a very modern museum mummy,
and the pesky geezer attached himself to me.
He said, We can't say what can't be said,
but damned if I won't take my licks.
I said, I hear you, buddy.
He said, Plowing up the football field
won't stop the game
but it will twist a lot of ankles.
I said, You know it, greybeard loon.
He said, They got a mouse up
in British Columbia that sneers
at everyone he sees.
I said, I hate that attitude.
He said, Never promise
your teachers you'll stay in touch.
I said, It's sad, but who has the time?
He said, You could make masks
of ancient Romans puking wine
with red strings that shoot
out of their mouths.
I said, Yes, but please, don't.
I climbed on top of the fridge
to get away from him.
He got on my kitchen counter-top.
He said, That dark day on the harbor
When white-capped water crashed the pier
A man in black danced tai-chi katas.
Mallards rode the swells.
A towering gray battleship cruised northward,
the crew lined the deck at attention
While high above circled a flock of big birds,
Not gulls, not pigeons. What were they?
I said, maybe turkey vultures?
He said, Buzzards don't circle the harbor.
I said, Let's get the guide and look them up.
Maybe they were cormorants.
Or angels.

The Tergiversations of Lux DeLite

In even his halcyon heydays
Seers always say Lux is headed for hell
And now their hair's on fire again

New one! new one! he shouts over the traffic
Crematogaster lineolata
Also known as acrobat ants

Never seen before on Broadway
Riding ponies sidesaddle
In the festival of logos parade

Seven hundred fifty species of fig tree
Each with its own pollinating wasp
And kilted piper keening

Let Lux be cold seawater for awhile
Clean and clear over granite rocks
No? okay, forget it

His basement cavern in the rain
His wretched shelter
His blue tarp sags and falls

A guest at a stranger's house
Swimming book in hand
He strays into the pool next door

White marble statuary
Neoclassical décor
He trespasses on some god's ground

So what if Lux be damned
He climbs the iron idols
Puts saltines in the mouths of the avatars

He rejects all gods that demand worship
And deeply suspects the devout
Of bowing before their own belief

Is he villainous? clever? he smiles
At his captors and slides
Face down the ice slick bridge

Across the frozen pond
To aright himself with ease
And stare his seers down

My Sin

The cellphone tower blew like a flower
Waved in the wind bowed her petals down
A silvery stranger chatting up the neighbors

She was no bombshell but she led with her chin
And I helplessly followed with my forehead
The motel man said you can't fake the mattress tag

No substitutions will be accepted
But I said look my name's right there
Inspected by P Smith

She read it and laughed
Your name's dumb
Still you know how to say it

In bed by a barbershop and fish sandwich stand
We were spotted in flagrante
Yet nobody was ashamed but me

She said they skimped on the skate
Late for work at eleven I scrambled
To reclaim my shoes and my videos

Out of a barrel a man was pulling
Fish with coiling tails I said I want a big one
He showed me how to slide

A knife beneath the spiky armored plates
To separate the flesh and I sliced up
His polo shirt instead

You bet that made me nervous
but didn't seem to faze the guy
Maybe he wasn't really a fishmonger

A truck pulled up at Christmas time
Towing automatic grottoes on wheels
Pre-fab piles of stones for prayer

That plug right in to your couch
Like an instant confessional box
Just add a priest or maybe don't

How I Feel About Cigars

The rock star of artisanal ham
Jimmy can't paint it purple until he owns it.
He made a black bundle of happy
Snapshots to be found in the wreck of his car.
He made black hair with
All the colors in the box.

The hot occupier said a train is coming
And we'll need a barrier.
Judy picked up a highway guard rail,
Wrapped scaffolding in plastic film
Propped everything up with paper.

Jimmy didn't want to stop the train
In fact he had to get on it
But he admired Judy's technique
He said where are you going later
Judy said Room O
She said she dressed for the party
like she was out to buy duct tape
You could tell Jimmy was after her
when Judy bicycled away
all his street signs fell down

Jimmy was almost immobilized
by a nauseating tension
between the spirit to keep going
and fear of failing without even knowing

His Car, His Bed, His Christmas Tree

His new shift is to care for dinosaur bones
He says I'm winging it best I can
Is it all I've ever, always on the fly
I say the answer never satisfies

An old bathtub Volvo to disassemble
Comes apart an antique brass bed
A family memento he says all sympathetic
I say no way we're buying this car
So mom sends us to get a Christmas tree
Out there naked past the fairgrounds with nothing but a hatchet
He says you don't know the real me nobody does
Probably a good thing I say
Keeps me chipper
Do you see anything remotely like a spruce

King queen and baby are nouns
I say to the baby what is a verb
Moving and changing the baby says
A paper pavilion of towers and pennants
Cascading drapery and tiny buttons
I stole them and will not give them back

He says my body is beginning to break
Still I don't feel adult inside
At my best a bright boy
And at your worst I say
Chin up and run with it

Outcomes are what we call them now
A narrow tunnel tighter than ever he says
Toward bright day to some sandcastle I suppose
Surrounded by aging acquaintances in time
For an acolyte actor to recite a sutra and sob a bit
At water's edge it works he says it's powerful
And maybe dangerous
Let's do it again

Obsessive, the Cowboy

Resist the urge to explain, Tex. Nobody's asking
about your swerve away from stickiness. You
were never quite correct. Drop something? Leave it!
Never go onto the tracks. Maybe wasted time is never wasted.
What if life is inescapably spent on experiences
we don't get right off the bat? Feelings suck up so much oxygen.
I don't know enough or do enough. My eye isn't blue enough—dude.
He's obsessive, the cowboy, she said to her gal pal.
Her boyfriend? Alone on the prairie, horse for companion,
out mending fences with meticulous care,
and she's calling him neurotic.
I feel you, Tex. Stay strong.

The View from Sturges Corner

*Glaciers can carry pretty much anything
they want. But which way did the glaciers go?*
Robert Titus, *The Catskills in the Ice Age*

We are city dwellers craving summer
Woods and wildflower fields so
Off we go when life allows
                and friends invite
We don't hesitate, we take
No time to acclimate
To the leafy green forest cats
I have named Little Jimmy and Long James
Whose stony spines rise above a valley
Carved by blue flowing ice
Twelve thousand years ago
We took our tall boy on a little tour:
front porch, barn, garden, apple tree,
hammock, lily pond and long expanses
of green and green and green
climbing up the mountainside
We set up on a table in the shade
With books and paints, we watched
Late afternoon sun and westerly breeze
Paint the waving branches of willow trees
I read what catty Catullus had to say
about his tortured love for a fickle girlfriend
and some jerk who stole his favorite napkins
The air grew cooler
We put on long pants
Sat by a fire in a pyramid stove
Watched the Dipper slowly brighten
Till we got sleepy
Went upstairs and let a bat out of the room
I dreamed I was cutting my hair
In the open air at a drive-in movie
I plugged my clippers into the speaker box
Dense clumps of hair clogged the blades

A man who wanted a cut
Asked to borrow the clippers
I said they're broken but
I'll rent them out
He gave me a look
Bees and butterflies enjoy
the wild thyme beside the path
We forage yellow gold chanterelles
from a pine forest I won't say where
Soft music of supple leaves
Summer society of trees
So talented at reflecting
our bodies and our moods
Trunks, limbs, seeds, sap
Reach, bend, wave, droop,
Whisper, sigh, sing, moan,
Grow bare, lean, fall down
Bright open gates to
Endless kickball summer
Climbing sycamore and maple
This is a common story
In the formerly ice age Catskills
You may be thinking
Of other summers
And wondering if they
Had a similar story.
They did.

In the Mountains

What about a gutter helmet sounds funny
But useful as a guard against a medley
Of precipitated exhaust, leaf litter and crushed ice

That drove us south to the mountains
For grandeur you don't find in the flats
Plus the lure of a live wire to jumpstart the juices

But sylvan silence can bug me
As much as overheard talk of deductibles.
Birdsong, please, or I'm cranking up-tempo jangle.

A trio of black capped chickadees
Chased through still bare branches
A little crested grey dude in the tulip trees

Sirens sang from the city below
A chill dropped in on me, a lifelong child
Wandering or pursued, a pilgrim not a pilgrim

A time traveler like you
The gods have always hung out on the heights,
hurling bolts from the blue and hollering

So that says something about what it takes to hear
the tiniest violet blossoms barely there
singing very quietly

Janus in Pajamas

At the window first thing
Half-light, streetlamps out
Quiet but for shifting gears
The uniform delivery truck
Returning from the hospital

Dead winter doldrums
Are just a disguise
Life wears when there's
Not enough sun
To be glad for no good reason

Yet life pulses behind
A skeleton mask
Singing almost silently
In praise of emptiness

Sun arrives, a gull cries
To pigeons spiraling a steeple

Dear Tomorrow

Dear Tomorrow, I am thinking of you
And join in the hope of your full recovery
Here at the Halfway House Motor Court we are beset
By overlapping structural problems
Our gang has plans to machine gun the Bankers Trust
Or maybe we skip the bullets and just do the ether
Though the game may be table tennis I say
Move the table and let's get down
For they also serve who stand and wait
With a red plastic shampoo bottle for a paddle

I vacuum and vacuum the gritty corners
Though the dust is really us
On the slow march back from Whateverland
Where the mothership has long sailed
Leaving us the Pleasures of the Harbor
Tattoo and Tanning Brew Pub
And a faint whiff of liberation
That comes with learning
That if nobody cares what one thinks
One can think whatever one likes

Voiceover Artist

His dream wakes him
I am the half-dead monkey
In the plastic bag, he says
Explaining it to himself
I say, Who are we but screens
Upon which we misread ourselves
Taking cues and mistaking clues
I disabled the memory
Of the graveyard TV, he says
I say, I thought it was you
I have seen flying clouds
Curling in arabesque
Predictably unbalanced yet
Nonetheless entertaining
He says, I am the man
With the alligator head
Snatching fish from the trash
I say, Let's walk across
This frozen lake of blueberry mousse
Like two perfect slices of multigrain toast
Popped up in a Proctor Silex
He says, I am the long gone glacier
The tide of grinding ice
I say, that's perfect
We'll mix two parts memory
One part desire, add bitters
And share the slanting light

He sleeps he is dreaming again
His face unwinds
An upturned cup of infinite sky
And so do I

Wintry Mix

I know I'm riding my bike upside down.
Gotta get off the red hibiscus cotton prints
hanging over the highway ramps
where angry white beaks and raisin eyes
weave around my windows.

It's Gleason again, jeez, I can't escape
the redundant brass buttons on his bus driver suit
as he climbs a brick chasm over rushing white water
to the stage where he does his bug-eyed shtick.

I want to live by the white water, too,
so I zoom in on the neighborhood map
and stroll there with wife and kids wondering
about the black smoke above the gorge

on our ritual return to a rock in a park,
a monument to god knows what
delicate disembodied hands flopping like fish
in a gutter to become a fur clad girl in fuzzy tights
and red Doc Martens. She smiles
and stacks bronze coins in my palm.

Now the train runs downstage instead of up
where the world is covered in pink wallpaper.
I hang my bike in a hole in the wall
and drape wet clothes by the window.

Last week's blizzard is crusty black
dumped from a rogue cement mixer
dawn through a lattice of clouds.

Toybox, jukebox, medicine chest,
crib to coffin chemistry set
to deep sigh in January sun.

At Her Service

The Frisbee coach poked me in the belly.
You're weak here, he said. Jesus
Had abs like a lion's.
That pissed me off. We were spotlighted
By sun through stained glass windows
Of scowling saints. I said, nice and loud
Over the ruckus from the choir loft,
Did you just say Jesus had abs?
That backed him off in a hurry.
Okay, don't get excited, he said.
I said, Take your hat off.

You can do a jig on somebody's grave.
The dead don't feel a thing.
We're always tromping over them,
Not just in the cemetery across from Midtown Elevator
And Times Trading Corporation. Somewhere
The dark bones of a big man
Are heaped on a sewer grate.

She was the ex-wife of a Band-Aid scion, actually.
Sitting in an attic in Rhinebeck, a statuette
Carved out of sardonyx, nephrite and cachalong.
Also mahogany coffin fragments of czar provenance,
Another encrustation that required a scraper.

I had risen to a table beside two young princes
Peering at texts from their peers
In a walnut-paneled room where a waiter brought soup
That I spilled into my lap but I was unembarrassed
And discretely picked shellfish from my pants
While I watched a two-hundred-year-old turtle
Crawl into a corner beside a radiator.
I said, I hope you don't get cooked.
He said, The comfort of the same thing every day
Gives way to despair of the same thing every day,
And back again, especially my routine 4 p.m.
I'm-gonna-jump-out-of-my-skin feeling.
When I'm aware of keeping up
I know I'm left behind.
Otherwise I think I'm fine.

Or Dusty, Depending

I was driving to down to Cincinnati in my baby, my trusty little Valium-yellow Fiat, when the song "Sunny" came on the radio. Dusty Springfield was singing, "you smiled at me and really eased the pain" and I felt like I was really digging it for the first time in my life so I didn't notice that the humpback bridge I drove onto was as insanely steep as a rollercoaster, going up, up, and up. I couldn't see anything but sky till I went over the top and my stomach dropped. Then I was going down way too fast toward a jumble of unmarked exit ramps. I jerked the wheel at the first right and before I knew it I hurtled over the guard rail. Zoom, wham, splash, there I was in the river, strangely still in one piece when I realized the water was so shallow I could stand up. What happened to Dusty Springfield? Where was my car? Over there on her side, poor thing, so small and wet, I picked her up, cradled her in my arms, and carried her to shore. And ever after I called my car Sunny. Or Dusty, depending.

My Man Sydney

what lit the urgent fire
in the gorge below
a random spark in

the heat and drought
did it rise from fissures
in sun bleached rock

mused Sydney Strange
of the Antiques Exchange
(417 Third Avenue, N.Y. 16, N.Y.)

while he tried to sleep
the façade fell off the wall
a rumble of limestone masonry

toy hands and heads of Della
Robbia baby dolls dropped
like exiled angels on the doorstep

what is a cherub's life anyhow
awful flying toddlers says Sydney
too holy for true

why not turn into a tree
it would be no tragedy
we do it all the time

or be the grandmother goddess
a seer in the racket of traffic
on Rector and West

her throne a battered club chair
her face a withered apple
her hair glossy black

presiding, dignified
in a fiery red pants suit
beside a hot dog vendor

whom Sydney presumes
is her dutiful grandson
preserving the flame

One Ring Circus

Her teeterboard
her trampoline
her Spanish web
her cannonball
how could I resist
her electromagnetic smile
her eyes that dared you to
Watch This
before she bounced
and flipped
and spun
and flew

She rode away
on her circus pony
her clown by her side
out of my life forever
Well, never in my life
She was a back-page obituary
my refuge when
the front is too much
as, woops, down we go
in thrall to another maniac
and my stomach does a flip

Come back angel acrobat
Our movie needs a special stunt
You hurtle into the oval office
deliver a flying kick in the face
to the dunce behind the desk
and disappear in a cloud of glitter
before the guards can grab you

Your Faithful Observer

Was it my fate to stay on the edge
of the action? A little bit unrealized?
Not for lack of trying. I always dive in.
That's my Achilles heel or my lunch
break talking. I settled my accounts
at the cigar store and bought a last
raggedy little stogie that fell apart
in my mouth. Isn't it time we took
off our glasses and slathered on
the slippery stuff? Before that guy
gets us all killed? Yes? No? As
you will, here at the Cocoa Bar,
Comrade.

I thought you were dead, baby,
half buried in the basement. You
always said it was your favorite room.
I watched and when you moved I called
out to the dance class, She's alive!
Not a glance in my direction.

We're all of us traumatized, Uncle.
Why don't you wash your hair?
He jumps in the lagoon with all that
busted lumber and poisonous muck
and we have to go after him.
Note to self: derm bundles
with a focus on antifungals.
Get in front of that snowball.

As it unfolded I got up to get off
the boat but we had already left the pier

You Might

You might cross a stage to greet
a beautiful character who says, You look healthy!
as though somebody is sick.
You might take her hand and murmur,
It's the best we can expect, isn't it?
You might drape a fleecy cape
across your chest and sit on a couch.
You might worry about packing your bags for a big trip
fully aware that your chest of drawers is part of the set.
You might decide it could wait.
You might proclaim, In France, one has morals or one does not!
Or maybe marbles.
You might leave it at that.
You might exit amidst silent derision.
You might be relieved to find a pony
waiting in the in the wings.

It always helps to have a pony
waiting in the wings.

Agar Agar Flipped Me Out

I woke up and felt weird about myself,
shamefully obvious, utterly predictable.
So I went to breathe deeply
at the underwater rummage sale,
to chat with bubbly church ladies,
and keep an eye on diving tigers.

For instance I dreamed I killed an intruder,
a sparrow in my mother's room,
by pressing a ballpoint against its throat.
I put it in a tissue and tossed it
at the door of the old chicken coop
where we cousins used to play as kids.
I was like that sometimes,
mixing memory with door solutions,
but my girlfriend wouldn't let me play
it for more than a millisecond—
what is that, turn it off, I hate that, she said.
No person, firm, corporation or association
could import, manufacture, sell or distribute
a yo-yo waterball. It was the law.

We gave a party against such gloom
and soon as Peg and Chip arrived from their hike
we went next door to Monty's duck pond.
He was practicing with his snorkel when I
began to worry about our other guests,
the junk food and blood sports,
but there was no going back,
the road petered out to a dirt track and left
me heartsick at the bottom of another
ravine. And my arms were so tired.

It was moving again. And hard. Nobody
could believe it. I could believe it.
I had to tread carefully.
The daycare said to go barefoot more often
but not in this highschool sockhop, no way.
I stole somebody's shoes,
got stuck in the mud
and had to self-extricate.

Summer Monday

On that holy day of observation
Harmonic Convergence? Uncles' Day?
We were late to join the circle
Cross-legged on someone's damp lawn
I bumped your knee sorry
And waited when Teddy got up to tell
Why the blender wasn't working properly
A nice little birdy zipped by in dipping arcs
No common robin or starling
Until the spell, such as it was, was broken
And it began to lightly rain
Once we put the picnic out
The kids drifted away to their usual pursuits
What is it they do anyway we wondered
Knowing full well and wanting some too
Since they'd be like us soon enough
Hands in our laps forgetting
What we were going to say
Oh yes what kind of bird was that
Later at the campfire my soul
A squarish glowing blob of stuff on a stick
Came out of my chest
I shared it around
And hoped for the best

A Little Radioactive Cube Of Black

explosive that powers the coffee machine
slowly poisons us but we need it
at home and the office we have to
take it to Ohio and bury it

I run a daycare center where
there are no kids at present
we are open for visits from prospective
parents and those who want to see
an antique camera in a glass vitrine

a window with a view back in time
I can't get started tho' I know
the routine: conventional wisdom, an opposing view,
then wacky word from a nut job what
a relief to wake to the Old English word
for swimming, sund, sund, sund

the pool is crowded with bumping
swimmers and lines of water walkers I must
move to the big pool and swim without
my boots on where to my surprise I can
hold my breath underwater forever but
afraid of rapture of the deep you
apparently bliss out then lose
consciousness I'm already spooked
at one remove when I surface to see
the water has drained from the pool

and dad asks if I have my Next Card

Harvest Of Hail

I insist there are too many corn cribs
for this little town to actually accommodate.
Somebody's up to no good.

Around the corner from the truck stop
on the crumbling porch of a defunct general store
I poke at the opaque control panel

and return to my boarding house room where
other lodgers are genial if somewhat confused
about what I can do with their old phonograph records.

Skipping school from forgetfulness is bad enough
but I'm the teacher. I sit on a low throne like a sage
to discuss the lesson of Lot's wife

who looks back at Yahweh's fire and brimstone
bombing her hometown and loses her life. Who
can blame her for one last glance?

I pick my barefoot way back home
leaving bloody prints from a cut on my toe
on busted brick and splintered board

to duck through dim makeshift sheds
where old men grumble and big boys boast.
I locked up my bike but forgot where I left it.

On the cusp of spring still digging
holes in the snow I punch my shovel
to the basement below and look

for stumps to stack to hold up the roof
as late winter gathers its clouds and gusts
for another swipe.

New Season

I was in the cheap seats behind the popcorn
stand where only the drunks and half-wits sit.
Couldn't see the show but the beach
was close by and out of the surf
came a "sandhog" like a little anteater,
its mouth a wide vacuum cleaner
of corrugated fiberglass. It snapped
at my ankles but I warded it off with a beer
can and listened to his gritty song,
some kind of advice about not having
to change your identity: In America
they considered us bums,
underachievers at best,
but I was absolutely alive
on a workday morning street,
free to be whoever I wanted
under the hood to do the necessary
repairs. I went at it with my electric
toothbrush but I needed a new
head. When I politely inquired
of the big woman behind the hardware
counter she said it's a shame
you don't understand the algorithms
that run your life. How well I knew
she meant make money from higher math
and I said the hell with moving the needle,
you sew a seam or get stuck,
screw the risk scores,
the clinical drivers, the prying drones.
If God led Mr. Hyde to Venetian Hills
I'm a monkey's uncle. I'm happy to lie
down on a big swing and spin
in slow circles. It's still very squishy
but there are a lot of interesting people,
migrating loons at lunch in the harbor,
tiny scarlet buds of a flowering cherry,
winking and smiling its branches
lovely knees and elbows flexing
in a breeze that is beginning
to feel a little too cold
for April.

Battery Gardens

A little soccer on the back lawn?
said the stroller most likely a mom.
A mismatch of downstream intent,
said the apologetic account exec.
Cue the blazing magnolias.
When I lament how
my time could be better spent
I wonder who would pay for it?
I'd love to linger here along the esplanade,
Peggy Sue, but like that guy who stopped
by a snowy woods and wished
he could fall down dead in a drift,
I've got obligations.
She said what's the trick but trying,
before giving up to admire
a brick-red tugboat straight outta Little Toot
and toot it did, a long tenor saxophone honk
as it rounded the harbor by Battery Park.
She wanted to follow that boat
to the ocean, dark and deep.

They settled for a selfie
with the Statue of Liberty.

Sometimes

Sometimes when I lie awake
in a black hole at a quarter to four
I hear an old car banging along
and I smell newsprint and ink
of fat Sunday Cincinnati Enquirers
bundled and banked on the back seat
like bolster pillows, fresh baked loaves
that invited a sleepy boy to doze
while my father feverishly drove
dark so dark through the snow.
Though he paid me to lend a hand,
to gather an armful, to trudge and throw,
sometimes he would let me be
and sleep, so sweetly sleep.

As a child I dreamed more than once
that my mom had lost her mind
to walk aimlessly along railroad tracks
absent from her wandering eyes,
but she didn't, her mind remained fine
though sometimes I'm afraid
I may lose mine
before I can act in time.
Laugh it off is all I can do.
Get on with life and lend a hand
while the next wave rolls in and subsides.

In Exurbia

He said the robot replicants
at the lakeside resort were poor
quality. Not smart? I asked. No,
slavish and superficially happy.
Not all of us, I said. For the sake
of variety I'm programmed
to be a sullen malcontent.
I was messing with him—
I didn't think I was a robot. But
when I heard about the attack
on the robot dog, I got nervous.
Would they suspect me? I snuck
out the backyard to the alley

and into a night of grand gestures,
messy, complicated, rapidly
deteriorating moments.
He splashed artisanal vinegar
made by Buddhist monks all over
the table and across the floor.
She lost control of her entrée,
the ravioli just up and ran away.
In bitterness, he blamed the food,
while detonating explosions
of fioratura at other Litchfield County
equestrian industries. Also
a winery in Argentina.

You tamp the box, play
with the lighter, you can exhale
and gaze into the middle
distance and look like
you're not hallucinating.
The company doesn't have anybody
who can, you know, delve back
into what we were thinking
when we did the schizophrenia ad.
I move about like an ordinary person.
Flowers are good listeners.

Make It Old

Make it old and a little fucked up
the way everything is that lasts
ancient, alive, smelly
subject to naked animal urges
however ridiculous it seems
to the young gods
so tragic in their taut ripeness

Make it old because we don't start fresh
but always with our catastrophe leftovers

Make it old as morning in a city alive
smells of cooking, cars, coffee, trees
newspapers, flowers, nasty colognes
a fleeting trace of happy
anticipation of even nothing new

Make it old as inevitable coincidence
(so funny at just that moment
I was thinking about you too)
Old as aplomb got from stubborn persistence

Make it old as afternoon
sunlight in sycamore treetops
fresh thick paint
on a bright red truck
that says "Emerald" in black letters

Make it old as the end of October
old as the devil, old as the dead

Make it old as the sun going down every day
time breaking every promise
old as the hour of blue
when we wonder what it is
we'd rather do

For Sue

Generally I am loathe
to make pronouncements but
we live many lives in one
and I don't presume
that cheers up anybody else
but I'm glad because I need more
more fried calamari and soft shell crabs
more salt crack caramel
more poems by Charlie Simic
more clear crescent moons over
pink and gold horizons
more sapphire skies at nine p.m.
more glockenspiel hymns
from ice cream trucks distantly hymning
more of Sue beside me gently sighing
more swimming

Who Knew

Like some kind of Jesus
Stretched on a rack
It was play practice
I was arching my back
I was making a model
For a show about gods
Big bearded Zeus
Stretched on a cloud
The pieces were small
They kept falling apart
A little white room
No way in no way out

Mom said she thought
She was going to heaven
But now she doesn't
I said are you crazy
She said I mean today

Then that day came

I had to lose
You to know
Who to tell
My troubles to
My funny ideas
I'll tell you
Who knew

Liberty Of Ashes

What gladdens a smashed and reeling day
when another ice storm has had its way?
The return of the striped Orvieto Cathedral tug, that's what,
as it escorts a barge of exotic cargo:
fabulous fruit in rainbow hues never seen,
luscious fabrics from silver looms,
spices in flavors as yet undreamed,
illuminated bibles of bizarre beliefs,
pornography, cookbooks, oracular poems
or maybe just a load of plowed snow—
still good.

When I was five my grandpa would give me a dollar
to buy him a pack of Camels and me a candy bar
from the ladies at the Gillen Crow drugstore.

In grade three I was proud as could be
of the red helmet I got to wear as class fire marshal.
Nice little red badge, too.

Now I admire with some surprise
the delicate red embroidery of my skin.

I spend my hour by the heaving ice unless
somebody has my spot below the wall.
If you smell a pungent cigar of moderate price, it's me.
A fine aroma evoking the terroir
of historic Honduran plantations is not me.
Though a lunch hour in El Paraiso might be nice
I smoke by the ice.

Later That Afternoon

I was on the sidewalk with an almost empty case
when my carpenter friend said, "Cheese it, amigo."
I took the tip, went down the block. My arm
was grabbed by a very tall man, tight dark
hair flat above his brow. Plainclothes, I presumed.
"They'll sentence you to time served," he said.
That made no sense. "Let me go and I won't tell
a soul you wear a wig," I said.
"Is it really obvious?" he said, touching his temples.
"No, but I have an eye for such things," I said.
"I myself am a master of disguise, and thus I am not
whom you believe me to be."
He said, "Shit. I wish I was better at this job."
"Maybe it's time you did something else," I said.
"I'm 58 years old," he said. "Who else will have me?"
He began weeping softly. "I've still got two kids in school."
"Children can be a comfort in old age," I said.
"Don't make me look bad," he said. "Please, let's go downtown."
I gave him my best hankie—light blue, maroon border.
While he wiped his tears I unfurled my gigantic wings
and we lifted off into evening's dappled sky.

Another Day In Paradise

Think of dark days as single threads
In a fine fabric that weaves itself ever wider
I'd rather not be apologizing on the phone
About your off-formulary medications
My mom used to sing hanging sheets in the sun
What is the ratio of crust to crumb?

Why do I so hate disorder?
Dishes in the sink
A dump of black snow
Here's another fine mess, Stanley
Right in front of us
And I like it well enough

You, the guy in the garden
Chinning himself on the arbor
And the woman feeding pigeons her crusts
Come join us at the snack bar
Of my heart

Leonard

I was admiring the knees and elbows
Of my favorite crabapple until I nodded off.
I dreamed a big egg salad sandwich was sailing
Up the Hudson. When I opened my eyes
Leonard Duncil was sitting beside me.
Look at you, an old man snoozing on a bench, he said.
I'd hardly call it snoozing, I said. I was just lost in thought.
I hadn't seen Leonard, the neighborhood bad boy,
Since 9th grade. He hadn't aged—same long greasy
Hair and adolescent beard. Are you spying on me? I said.
If I'm a spy, I must be good, he said. You haven't seen
Me in thirty years. He had me there. Still I was
Suspicious. He said, You sit here moping until you see
Something you think is funny, like a truck for Giant Big
Apple Beer. I said, What's not funny about Giant Big
Apple Beer? Are you a ghost? Were you an evil pimp,
Murdered by one of your whores? He said, Wow.
I'm an aircraft engineer and a grandpa. I don't look like
This anymore. Why do you remember me? I said, Blue
Print Cleanse. We Think. You Drink. That's funny isn't it?
He said, You and your sisters were straight out of the Brady
Bunch. I said, You were a happy delinquent. I was a lonely nerd.
I gathered Leonard Duncil into my arms
As the crabapple waved in the June breeze.

To My New Pal Li Po

Furtive flicker pauses on birch top
Disappears with his red spot
One monarch butterfly lights
On granite shoulder flecked with green lichen
Flashing orange wings lift it away
Years ago there were so many

My daughter leaves on the ferry tomorrow
Now she sits where the butterfly was
Her knees at her chin, pretending to smile
Blue heron gliding over blue water
A cello note low over flutes of tide

Jupiter

I see Jupiter just before dawn
So fat I think it's a helicopter hovering
Over bad traffic on the expressway
Until I look through my glasses
Good news for the morning commute
No tie ups on the Gowanus
A big planet in plain view
While we swing into sunlight

I push my father, not so old but frail,
In a rolling recliner chair
On small wheels up a steep street
Bumping over sidewalk seams
As dusk falls and windows light

He gives me a tiny box, a kit
To make to make a matchbook house,
Like Tinker Toy sticks the size of splinters
He warns me not to spill them

I leave him in his living room
On a low pallet beside a TV
He says we'll meet at the flea market

I carry two light cases of his odds and ends
Out into the night and unfamiliar blocks
Lost as it begins to rain but stops

I take a wrong turn up cemetery steps
And cannot get back down
For the crowds of people climbing

Urgent

the time is out of joint
the time is ripe
the time is now
the time is running out
the time my wallet fell into a sewer
and two panhandlers dangled me
by the legs to fish it out
I am past my bow-tied heyday
a shiny little bomb in a jewel box
awaiting my turn to detonate
now I repair teakettles, sonny
and grateful to get the work
back to the dream farm
all sun and tall corn
rusty red tractor, falling down barn
acutely aware of something
big wrapped in burlap
hiding just out of sight
still I am happy, so happy
to be visiting home
my sisters and cousins
still kids telling dreams
cracking up over our Cheerios
I take my joy
where I can find it
let it bubble up
from my heart to my head
and wash me over I will
remember it when I wake

Wichita Lineman Sutra

"I hear you singing in the wire"
The varied carols I hear
People who can come across as space
Cases if you know the backstory
Bowl-cuts, buzz-cuts, frohawks, fades
Kind of a kick-ass yearning
Toward the ineffable soul, that drop, that ray
Rescued after six days in a Houston manhole

"Searching in the sun for another overload"
A low-frequency sizzle, smell of a new Band-Aid
Like the year I had chicken pox on Halloween
Remember? The blue princess gown
I didn't get to wear. You sweetly shared
Your candy. Spread it out on a sheet
Even let me have some good stuff
Bit O'Honey and Mary Jane
Peanut Butter Kisses
I remember your face

"And if it snows that stretch down south"
Is gonna snap like an old rubber band
O snow is so yesteryear, they came
With a rainmaker to soak our parade
Still the girls rocked out under the trees
Directly atop a whorl of foliage
Flushes of magenta pink at your throat

Hi, Daddy. Are you about to take a nap?
We won! Wasn't it a great game?

About the author

Pat Smith is a writer living in New York City. His MFA is from NYU's Tisch School of the Arts and his play *Driving Around the House*, produced around the U.S., is published by New Rivers Press. His poems have appeared in online journals, most recently in *Across the Margin*. This book is his first published collection.

www.ingramcontent.com/pod-product-compliance
Lightning Source LLC
Chambersburg PA
CBHW022000290426
44108CB00012B/1146